How is it so easy for you to screw people?
she asked
milk and honey dripped
from my dick as I answered
cause people have not screwed me

The first girl I kissed
I held her shoulder like a handlebar of bicycle
In reaction, she twisted my balls
I screamed in pain

Milk and Honey Parody: Grab Her By the Pusheen and Other Poetries

Milk and Honey Parody: Grab Her By the Pusheen and Other Poetries

INTRODUCTION
ABOUT AUTHOR

This book is dedicated to all Americans.

Disclaimer: All characters, companies, events, places mentioned in the book are purely fictitious, any similarity with a person or company or event or place is purely coincidental.

Introduction

This book is written for all Americans who love poetry and Donald trump. Please stop reading unless you have got good sense of humor.

My dick woke me up last night
How I can help, I begged
My dick said
Go get some girl and
Grab her by the pusheen

She had the smell of
milk and honey on her lips
which she picked up while eating
milk and honey at breakfast
and did I feel hungry
as she felt before eating her breakfast

*I was taught that there was a pit stop for men
between the legs of women
I did not know, I had to mortgage my ass
to take care of the luxury between the legs*

I must have known
it was wrong to finger someone against her will
no honey came out of it
she kicked me in the mouth
it broke my teeth

Semen is water
soft enough to give life
tough enough to kill germs

Our dicks
tell stories
none has the pushene to publish

I did not leave because
I stopped loving you
I just found someone hotter

You are fired
I whispered
as you rammed the door on my face

You were not my first love
every time I make love with you
All my past lovers surface in my mind

The very thought of you
gets my dick erected
like an bee looking for honey

I am not an ATM.
I am a man.
I am not a shopping Mall
I do not earn enough to afford luxury.
stop forcing me to pay for your perversions
else your lazy ass is fired

The idea that we are
so capable of making love
but still choose
to not make it
makes a man go for another man

I do not want to have you
for emptying my pockets
I want you to earn what you need
else you are fired

*The next time she points out that
you are no longer performing like a porn-star
remind her that it's your body
the body is aging
she is just a guest
warn her to stay in her limit*

*If you are bankrupt
and she left you
do not repent
she was not yours at very first place*

You can love your self
you can make love with your self
if you want to be happy in life
do not depend on others for love

At the end of day
your degree, job, money, etc. does not matter
it only matters whether you have got a young
and beautiful ass
to make love with

What is stronger than human heart which
shatters again and again but lives?
It's the dick

Loneliness is a sign you need to masturbate

*The beauty in me is that I am very rich
all women flirt with me
to get grabbed by the Pusheen*

Women can be ugly inside and outside
They can cause lot of pain
do not be afraid of pain
it can turn your charcoal into a diamond
else just turn Gay

The kindest words my girlfriends said to me
men like you can fill a swimming pool using dick

People say things to rip you apart
your mind can the stop them to enter your heart.
use it wisely to ignore them.

About Author

John Trumpet is bestselling author of "Milk and Honey Parody: Grab Her By the Pusheen and Other Poetries". If you would like to publish this book in your country, please feel free to contact at johntrumpet_@outlook.com.